A Little Volume,
but Great Book.
— CRASHAW

The LITTLE BOOK OF FRIENDSHIP

Compiled and Edited
with an Introduction by
Wallace and Frances Rice

Publishers
THE REILLY & BRITTON CO.
Chicago

Introduction

I T IS a curious fact that, while Friendship has been properly described as the master passion, and certainly plays a master part in the daily business of the world, Friendship in the abstract has never yet inspired a poem of the first magnitude and importance. Friendship in a concrete form, especially the grief felt at the loss of a friend, has given the English language a series of threnodies which are not to be paralleled in any tongue. Yet these, on the closest examination, will be found to say almost nothing about the abstract passion, limiting themselves strictly to lamentation over the friend who has gone.

Epic poetry can hardly be said to exist without the expression of the final necessity for a man's having friends; yet it is quite as true here that the feeling shown is for the individual beloved, and not for that more universal sentiment by which all friends in all times and places are governed. Shelley bewails the untimely taking off of Keats, Tennyson mourns the death of Hallam, Virgil is for ever talking of the faithful Achates; yet neither in ''Adonaïs,'' in ''In Memoriam,'' nor in the Æneid is there any praise of Friendship as such. And this is equally true of the drama: Damon and Pythias may have their mutual and most sweet devotion duly staged, but Damon is Damon to Pythias, and not Friendship personified. It seems to be true that the greatest Friendships are, like Love, selfish and egotistic, a mere projection of self.

3

In consequence, the contents of this book are in good part the expression of individual Friendship, tempered by a large proportion of abstract poems, in which the authors appear to have had a real gift for Friendliness, and by reason of it to have learned the beauties and divinities of this serene and spiritual human passion — something seemingly impossible to those whose whole devotion is engaged by an individual.

But this has not deterred the prose writers, from Cicero to our own Emerson, from setting forth the glories and beauties of Friendship in a manner that leaves one amazed at the poets' neglect. For, after all, Friendship is the universal solvent or alkahest for every evil the world sorrows over. Between man and man it strips the soul from every vestige of sordidness and brings — as between true friends, at least — the Golden Rule into realization. Extended from man to the State, it would solve all the vexed problems of civilization. Yet even this magnificent conception of the possibilities of Friendship has not, so far, made its appeal to the poet's heart, much as the great teachers of religion have insisted upon it. For true Friendship is religious and of the very essence of piety.

WALLACE RICE.

Index Of Authors

The LITTLE
BOOK OF
FRIENDSHIP

It is a sweet thing, friendship, a dear balm,
A happy and auspicious bird of calm
Which rides o'er life's ever-tumultuous ocean:
A god that broods o'er chaos in commotion;
A flower which fresh as Lapland roses are,
Lifts its bold head into the world's frore air,
And blooms most radiantly when others die,
Health, hope, and youth, and brief prosperity;
And with the light and odor of its bloom,
Shining within the dungeon and the tomb;
Whose coming is as light and music are
'Mid dissonance and gloom — a star
Which moves not mid the moving heavens alone,
A smile amid dark frowns — a gentle tone
Among rude voices, a belovéd light,
A solitude, a refuge, a delight.

— Percy Bysshe Shelley.

Flowers are lovely; Love is flower-like;
    Friendship is a sheltering tree;
O the joys that came down shower-like,
    Of Friendship, Love, and Liberty,
            Ere I was old!
                — Samuel Taylor Coleridge.

The
Little Book of Friendship

Friendship

A ruddy drop of manly blood
The surging sea outweighs,
The world uncertain comes and goes;
The lover rooted stays.
I fancied he was fled —
And, after many a year,
Glowed unexhausted kindliness,
Like daily sunrise there.
My careful heart was free again,
O friend, my bosom said
Through thee alone the sky is arched,
Through thee the rose is red;
All things through thee take nobler form,
And look beyond the earth,
The mill-round of our fate appears
A sun-path in thy worth.
Me too thy nobleness has taught
To master my despair;
The fountains of my hidden life
Are through thy friendship fair.

— Ralph Waldo Emerson.

Friendship's the wine of life.—Edward Young.

Friendship

Friendship, peculiar boon of heaven,
   The noble mind's delight and pride,
To men and angels only given,
   To all the lower world denied.

While love, unknown among the blest,
   Parent of thousand wild desires,
The savage and the human breast
   Torments alike with raging fires.

With bright, but oft destructive gleam,
   Alike o'er all his lightnings fly,
Thy lambent glories only beam
   Around the favorites of the sky.

Thy gentle flows of guiltless joys,
   On fools and villains ne'er descend;
In vain for thee the tyrant sighs,
   And hugs a flatterer for a friend.

Directress of the brave and just,
   O guide us through life's darksome way!
And let the tortures of mistrust
   On selfish bosoms only prey.

Nor shall thine ardors cease to glow
   When souls to peaceful climes remove: —
What raised our virtues here below,
   Shall aid our happiness above.

                — Samuel Johnson.

A good friend is better than a near relation.

Friendship

Distilled amidst the gloom of night,
  Dark hangs the dew-drop on the thorn;
Till, noticed by approaching light,
  It glitters in the smile of morn.

Morn soon retires, her feeble power
  The sun out-beams with genial day,
And gently, in benignant hour,
  Exhales the liquid pearl away.

Thus on affliction's sable bed
  Deep sorrows rise of saddest hue;
Condensing round the mourner's head
  They bathe the cheek with chilly dew.

Though pity shows her dawn from heaven,
  When kind she points assistance near,
To friendship's sun alone 't is given
  To soothe and dry the mourner's tear.

— Thomas Penrose.

From "The Wants of Man"

I want a warm and faithful friend,
  To cheer the adverse hour;
Who ne'er to flatter will descend,
  Nor bend the knee to power.
A friend to chide me when I 'm wrong,
  My inmost soul to see;
And that my friendship prove as strong
  To him as his to me.

— John Quincy Adams.

From "Friendship"

I awoke this morning with devout thanksgiving
for my friends, the old and the new. Who hears me,
who understands me, becomes mine—a possession for
all time. Friendship, like the immortality of the soul,
is too good to be believed. Every man passes his
life in the search after friendship. Its laws are great,
austere, and eternal, of one web with the laws of
nature and of morals. Love, which is the essence of
God, is not for levity, but for the total worth of man.
Let us approach our friend with an audacious trust
in the truth of his heart, in the breadth, impossible to
be overturned, of his foundations.

I do not wish to treat friendships daintily, but with
roughest courage. When they are real, they are not
glass threads or frost-work, but the solidest things we
know. Happy is the house that shelters a friend!

There are two elements that go to the composition
of friendship, each so sovereign, that I can detect no
superiority in either, no reason why either should be
first named. One is Truth. A friend is a person with
whom I can be sincere. Before him, I may think
aloud. The other element of friendship is Tender-
ness. When a man becomes dear to me, I have touched
the goal of fortune. I wish that friendship should
have feet, as well as eyes and eloquence. It must
plant itself on the ground, before it walks over the
moon. I wish it to be a little of a citizen, before it is
quite a cherub. I hate the prostitution of the name of
friendship to signify modish and worldly alliances.
The end of friendship is a commerce the most strict
and homely that can be joined.—Ralph Waldo Emerson.

The Heart's Treasure

The scampering squirrel, when the Autumn's gift
  Of opening chestnuts and sweet mast descends,
  Bestows them in the keep the poplar lends
  Against the wind that sets the snows adrift;
And the lithe branches to the sunlight lift
  Their length unburdened now, each bough unbends
  And raises hands on high, till Heaven sends
  Their prayer its answer in the season's shift.

Even so my heart stores safe the tender smile,
  The kindly word, the gentle deed, of those
  Who are my friends against Time's drifting snows;
And still the tendrils of that heart reach forth
  And point me to the dear ones lost awhile
  Within the Spring beyond the frozen North.
                  — Wallace Rice.

Friend of my earliest years and childish days,
  My joys, my sorrows, thou with me hast shared,
  Companion dear, and we alike have fared
  (Poor Pilgrims we) through life's unequal ways;
It were unwisely done, should we refuse
  To cheer our path as featly as we may,
  Our lonely path to cheer, as travelers use,
  With merry song, quaint tale, or roundelay;
And we will sometimes talk past troubles o'er,
  Of mercies shown, and all our sickness healed,
  And in his judgments God remembering love;
And we will learn to praise God evermore
  For those great tidings of great joy revealed
  By that sooth messenger sent from above.
                  — Charles Lamb.

The House By the Side of the Road

There are hermit souls that live withdrawn
  In the place of their self-content;
There are souls like stars, that dwell apart,
  In a fellowless firmament;
There are pioneer souls that blaze their paths
  Where highways never ran —
But let me live by the side of the road
  And be a friend to man.

Let me live in a house by the side of the road
  Where the race of men go by —
The men who are good and the men who are bad,
  As good and as bad as I.
I would not sit in the scorner's seat
  Or hurl the cynic's ban —
Let me live in a house by the side of the road
  And be a friend to man.

I see from my house by the side of the road,
  By the side of the highway of life,
The men who press with the ardor of hope,
  The men who are faint with the strife,
But I turn not away from their smiles nor their tears,
  Both parts of an infinite plan —
Let me live in a house by the side of the road
  And be a friend to man.

I know where are brook-gladdened meadows ahead,
  And mountains of wearisome height;
That the road passes on through the long afternoon
  And stretches away to the night.

And still I rejoice when the travelers rejoice
　　And weep with the strangers that moan,
Nor live in my house by the side of the road
　　Like a man who dwells alone.

Let me live in my house by the side of the road,
　　It 's here the race of men go by —
They are good, they are bad, they are weak, they are
　　　　strong,
　　Wise, foolish — so am I.
Then why should I sit in the scorner's seat,
　　Or hurl the cynic's ban ?
Let me live in my house by the side of the road
　　And be a friend to man.

　　　　　　　　　— Sam Walter Foss.

Sonnet XXX

When to the sessions of sweet silent thought
　　I summon up remembrance of things past,
I sigh the lack of many a thing I sought,
　　And with old woes new wail my dear time's waste:
Then can I drown an eye, unused to flow,
　　For precious friends hid in death's dateless night,
And weep afresh love's long since canceled woe,
　　And moan the expense of many a vanished sight:
Then can I grieve at grievances foregone,
　　And heavily from woe to woe tell o'er
The sad account of fore-bemoanéd moan,
　　Which I new pay as if not paid before.
But if the while I think on thee, dear friend,
All losses are restored and sorrows end.

　　　　　　　　　— William Shakespeare.

Friendship

Friendship needs no studied phrases,
  Polished face or winning wiles;
Friendship deals no lavish praises,
  Friendship dons no surface smiles.

Friendship follows Nature's diction,
  Shuns the blandishments of Art,
Boldly severs truth from fiction,
  Speaks the language of the heart.

Friendship favors no condition
  Scorns a narrow-minded creed,
Lovingly fulfils its mission,
  Be it word or be it deed.

Friendship cheers the faint and weary,
  Makes the timid spirit brave,
Warns the erring, lights the dreary,
  Smooths the passage to the grave.

Friendship — pure unselfish friendship,
  All through life's allotted span,
Nurtures, strengthens, widens, lengthens
  Man's affinity with man.

———————

Friendship, like love, is but a name,
Unless to one you stint the flame.
The child whom many fathers share,
Hath seldom known a father's care.
'T is thus in friendships; who depend
On many, rarely find a friend.

— John Gay.

Friendship

Dear friend, I pray thee, if thou wouldst be proving
  Thy strong regard for me,
Make me no vows. Lip service is not loving;
  Let thy faith speak for thee.

Swear not to me that nothing can divide us,
  So little such oaths mean,
But when distrust and envy creeps beside us,
  Let them not come between.

Say not to me the depths of thy devotion
  Are deeper than the sea;
But watch, lest doubt of some unkind emotion
  Embittered them for me.

Vow not to love me ever and for ever,
  Words are such idle things,
But when we differ in opinions, never
  Hurt me by little stings.

I 'm sick of words, they are so lightly spoken
  And spoken but as air.
I 'd rather feel thy trust in me unbroken
  Than list to thy words so fair.

If all the little proofs of trust are heeded,
  If thou art always kind,
No sacrifice, no promise will be needed
  To satisfy my mind.

                    — Ella Wheeler Wilcox.

Keep thy friend thy better self.

From the Essay "Of Friendship"

A crowd is not company, and faces are but a gallery of pictures; and talk but a tinkling cymbal, where there is no love. In a great town friends are scattered, so that there is not that fellowship, for the most part, which is in less neighborhoods. But we may go farther and affirm most truly, that it is a mere and miserable solitude, to want true friends, without which the world is but a wilderness. Whosoever in the frame of his nature and affections is unfit for friendship, he taketh it of the beast, and not from humanity.

A principal fruit of friendship is the ease and discharge of the fullness and swelling of the heart, which passions of all kinds do cause and induce. No receipt openeth the heart but a true friend, to whom you may impart griefs, joys, fears, hopes, suspicions, counsels, and whatsoever lieth upon the heart to oppress it, in a kind of civil shrift or confession.

Those who want friends to open themselves unto, are cannibals of their own hearts. But one thing is most admirable, which is, that this communicating of a man's self to his friend works two contrary effects; for it redoubleth joys, and cutteth grief in halfs. For there is no man that imparteth his joys to his friends, but he joyeth the more; and no man that imparteth his griefs to his friend, but he grieveth the less.

Friendship maketh daylight in the understanding, out of darkness and confusion of thoughts; whosoever hath his mind fraught with many thoughts, his wits and understanding do clarify in discouraging with another; and that more by an hour's discourse, than by a day's meditation. — Francis Bacon, Lord Verulam.

To Thomas Moore

My boat is on the shore,
   And my bark is on the sea;
But before I go, Tom Moore,
   Here 's a double health to thee !

Here 's a sigh to those who love me,
   And a smile to those who hate;
And, whatever sky 's above me,
   Here 's a heart for every fate.

Though the ocean roar around me,
   Yet it still shall bear me on:
Though a desert should surround me,
   It hath springs that may be won.

Were 't the last drop in the well,
   As I gasped upon the brink,
Ere my fainting spirit fell,
   'T is to thee that I would drink.

With that water, as this wine,
   The libation I would pour
Should be: Peace to thine and mine,
   And health to thee, Tom Moore.
         — George Lord Byron.

A generous friendship no cold medium knows,
Burns with one love, with one resentment glows;
One should our interests and our passions be,
My friend must hate the man that injures me.
         — Alexander Pope.

A Sentiment

The pledge of Friendship! it is still divine,
Though watery floods have quenched its burning wine;
Whatever vase the sacred drops may hold,
The gourd, the shell, the cup of beaten gold,
Around its brim the hand of Nature throws
A garland sweeter than the banquet's rose.
Bright are the blushes of the vine-wreathed bowl,
Warm with the sunshine of Anacreon's soul,
But dearer memories gild the tasteless wave
That fainting Sidney perished as he gave.
'T is the heart's current lends the cup its glow,
Whate'er the fountain whence the draught may flow, —
The diamond dew-drops sparkling through the sand,
Scooped by the Arab in his sunburnt hand,
Or the dark streamlet oozing from the snow,
Where creep and crouch the shuddering Esquimaux;
Aye, in the stream that, ere again we meet
Shall burst the pavement, glistening at our feet,
And, stealing silent from its leafy hills,
Thread all our alleys with its thousand rills, —
In each pale draught if generous feeling blend,
And o'er the goblet friend shall smile on friend,
Even cold Cochituate every heart shall warm,
And genial Nature shall defy reform !
                              — Oliver Wendell Holmes.

Friendship is constant in all other things,
Save in the office and affairs of love:
Therefore all hearts in love use their own tongues;
Let every eye negotiate for itself,
And trust no agent: for beauty is a witch,
Against whose charms faith melteth into blood.
                              — William Shakespeare.

The Memory of the Heart

If stores of dry and learnéd lore we gain,
We keep them in the memory of the brain;
Names, things, and facts, — whate'er we knowledge
    call —
There is the common ledger for them all;
And images on this cold surface traced
Make slight impression, and are soon effaced,
But we 've a page, more glowing and more bright,
On which our friendship and our love we write;
That these may never from the soul depart,
We trust them to the memory of the heart.
There is no dimming, no effacement there;
Each new pulsation keeps the record clear;
Warm golden letters all the tablet fill,
Nor lose their luster till the heart stands still.

— Daniel Webster.

From "Friendship"

Thick waters show no images of things;
Friends are each other's mirrors, and should be
Clearer than crystal, or the mountain springs,
And free from clouds, design, or flattery.
For vulgar souls no part of friendship share;
Poets and friends are born to what they are.

— Catherine Philips.

Hand

Grasps hand, eye lights eye in good fellowship,
And great hearts expand,
And grow one in the sense of this world's life.

— Robert Browning.

From "De Amicitia"

Prefer friendship to all human possessions, for there is nothing so suited to our nature, so well adapted to prosperity or adversity. But, first of all, I am of opinion that except among the virtuous friendship cannot exist. Friendship is superior to relationship, because from kinship benevolence can be withdrawn, and from friendship it cannot; for with the withdrawal of benevolence the very name of friendship is done away, while that of kinship remains. Now how great the power of friendship is, may be best gathered from this, that out of the boundless society of the human race, which nature herself has joined together, friendship is a matter brought into so narrow a compass, that the whole of affection is confined to two, or at any rate to very few.

Now friendship is nothing else than a complete union of feeling on all subjects, accompanied by kindliness and attachment; than which, indeed, I am not aware whether, with the exception of wisdom, anything better has been bestowed upon man. Some prefer riches, others good health, others influence, others again honors, many prefer even pleasures: the last, indeed, is the characteristic of beasts; while the former are fleeting, depending on fortune. Those who place the supreme good in virtue, therein do admirably; but this very virtue itself both begets and constitutes friendship; nor without this virtue can friendship exists at all.

And while friendship possesses very many and great advantages, she undoubtedly surpasses all in this, that she shines with a brilliant hope over the future, and never suffers the spirit to sink. — Cicero.

In a Friendly Sort o' Way

When a man ain't got a cent, and he 's feeling kind
    of blue,
An' the clouds hang dark an' heavy an' won't let
    the sun shine through,
It 's a great thing, O my brethren, for a feller just
    to lay
His hand upon your shoulder in a friendly sort o' way!

It makes a man feel curious; it makes the tear drops
    start,
An' you sort o' feel a flutter in the region of the
    heart.
You can't look up and meet his eyes; you don't
    know what to say,
When his hand is on your shoulder in a friendly sort
    o' way.

Oh, the world 's a curious compound, with its honey
    and its gall,
With its cares an' bitter crosses; but a good world,
    after all,
An' a good God must have made it — leastways that 's
    what I say,
When a hand rests on my shoulder in a friendly sort
    o' way.   — James Whitcomb Riley.

Under the magnetism of friendship the modest man
becomes bold, the shy confident, the lazy active, or the
impetuous, prudent and peaceful. — William Makepeace
Thackeray.

    Ah, Friendship, stronger in thy might
    Than time and space, as faith than sight!
            — Helen Hunt Jackson.

I Like the New Friends Best

Old friends are 'most too home-like now.
They know your age, and when
You got expelled from school, and lots
Of other things, an' then
They 'member when you shivareed
The town an' broke the lights
Out of the school 'nen run away
An' played "Hunt Cole" out nights.
They 'member when you played around
Your dear old mommy's knee;
It's them can tell the very date
That you got on a spree.
I don't like to forget 'em, yet
If put right to the test
Of hankerin' right now for 'em,
I like the new friends best.

— Ben King.

From "Ben Bolt"

There is change in the things I loved, Ben Bolt,
  They have changed from the old to the new;
But I feel in the deeps of my spirit the truth,
  There never was change in you.
Twelve months twenty have passed, Ben Bolt,
  Since first we were friends; yet I hail
Your presence a blessing, your friendship a truth,
  Ben Bolt of the salt sea gale.

— Thomas Dunn English.

A day for toil, an hour for sport,
  But for a friend life is too short.

— Ralph Waldo Emerson.

24

Friendship's Wish

To grow old with you; when the days grow sere
To be beside you and make Time appear
    Our willing servant; at an age awry
    To laugh and jest, O friend, as weeks go by;
Renewing youth in friendship close and dear:

These leave the sweeter every hastening year;
Still is the earth green; and skies are ever clear
    That hearken to my happy heart's fond cry
        To grow old with you!

And how old joys return and linger here
In the retelling; how quickly dries the tear
    You smile upon; how fast the new griefs fly!
    So, when fulfilment comes, why, then shall I
Smile at my granted wish (how should I fear?)
        To grow old with you!
                                    — Wallace Rice.

A Friend in Need

        A friend in need? —
    When need we not a friend
    Some kindly aid to lend
        Our onward steps to speed?
        A friend in need
    Grant us till life shall end
        For happiness to plead,
        For grace to intercede.
    Daily we pray: God send
        A friend in need!

From "Ecclesiasticus"

Sweet words will multiply a man's friends; and a fair-speaking tongue will multiply courtesies. Let those that are at peace with thee be many; but thy counselors one of a thousand. If thou wouldest get thee a friend, get him by proving, and be not in haste to trust him. For there is a friend that is so for his own occasion, and he will not continue in the day of thy affliction. And there is a friend that turneth to enmity; and he will discover strife to thy reproach. And there is a friend that is a companion at the table, and he will not continue in the day of thy affliction; and in thy prosperity he will be as thyself, and will be bold over thy servants; if thou shalt be brought low, he will be against thee, and he will hide himself from thy face.

Separate thyself from thine enemies; and beware of thy friends. A faithful friend is a strong defence; and he that hath found him hath found a treasure. There is nothing that can be taken in exchange for a faithful friend; and his excellency is beyond price. A faithful friend is a medicine of life; and they that fear the Lord shall find him. He that feareth the Lord directeth his friendship aright; for as he is so is his neighbor also.

Entreat me not to leave thee, or to return from following after thee: for whither thou goest I will go; and where thou lodgest, I will lodge; thy people shall be my people, and thy God my God. Where thou diest, I will die, and there will I be buried; the Lord do so to me, and more also, if aught but death part thee and me. — From the book of Ruth.

No More but So?

No more but so? Only with uncold looks,
  And with a hand not laggard to clasp mine,
  Think'st thou to pay what debt of love is thine?
  No more but so? Like gushing water-brooks,
No more but so? Like gushing water-brooks,
Freshening and making green the dimmest nooks
  Of thy friend's soul, thy kindliness should flow;
  But, if 't is bounded by not saying "no,"
  I can find more of friendship in my books,
All lifeless though they be, and more, far more
  In every simplest moss, or flower, or tree;
  Open to me thy heart of hearts' deep core,
Or never say that I am dear to thee;
  Call me not Friend, if thou keep close the door
  That leads into thine inmost sympathy.

                  — James Russell Lowell.

"Count Me not Less"

Count me not less thy friend because my heart,
Blinded a moment by the light of youth,
Leaped toward thee ere it took thine estimate,
And knew no leap might carry it so high
As where thy heart beats lonely. Count me not
The less thy friend in that I love you, dear.

                  — Caroline Duer.

Friendship 's an abstract of this noble flame,
'T is love refined and purged from all its dross,
'T is next to angel's love, if not the same,
As strong in passion is, though not so gross.

                  — Catherine Philips.

From the Essay "Of Friendship"

There is nothing to which Nature hath more addressed us than to society. And Aristotle saith that perfect law-givers have had more regardful care of friendship than of justice. And the utmost drift of its perfection is this. For generally, all those amities which are forged and nourished by voluptuousness or profit, public or private need, are thereby so much the less fair and generous, and so much the less true amities, in that they intermeddle other causes, scope, and fruit with friendship, than itself alone.

According as they are friendships which the law and duty of nature doth command us, so much the less of our own voluntary choice and liberty is there required unto it. And our own liberty hath no production more properly her own, than that of affection and amity. In true friendship it is a general and universal heat, all pleasure and smoothness, that hath no pricking or stinging in it. Friendship is enjoyed according as it is desired; it is neither bred nor nourished, nor increaseth but in jouissance, as being spiritual, and the mind being refined by use and custom.

Common friendships may be divided; a man may love beauty in one, facility of behavior in another, liberality in one, and wisdom in another, and so forth; but this amity which possesseth the soul, and sways it in all its sovereignty, it is impossible it should be double. For a man shall easily find men fit for a superficial acquaintance; but in this, wherein men negotiate from the very center of their hearts, and make no spare of anything, it is most requisite that all the wards and springs be perfectly true. — Michel, Sieur de Montaigne.

28

From "The Joys of the Road"

A scrap of gossip at the ferry;
A comrade neither glum nor merry,

Asking nothing, revealing nought,
But minting his words from a fund of thought,

A keeper of silence eloquent,
Needy, yet royally well content,

Of the mettled breed, yet abhorring strife,
And full of the mellow juice of life,

A taster of wine, with an eye for a maid,
Never too bold, and never afraid,

Never heart-whole, never heart-sick
(These are the things I worship in Dick),

No fidget and no reformer, just
A calm observer of ought and must,

A lover of books, but a reader of man,
No cynic and no charlatan,

Who never defers and never demands,
But, smiling, takes the world in his hands, —

Seeing it good as when God first saw
And gave it the weight of His will for law.
                    — Bliss Carman, to Richard Hovey.

A Thanksgiving

Long enough have I lived and sought to know the
    value of things,
To know the gold from the tinsel, to judge the clowns
    from the kings;
Love have I known and been glad of, joys of the earth
    have been mine,
But to-day do I give my thanks for a rarer gift and
    fine:

For the friendship of good women, Lord, that hath
    been since the world hath breath,
Since a woman stood at a woman's side to comfort
    through birth and death.
You have made us a bond of mirth and tears to last
    for ever and ay —
For the friendship of true women, Lord, take you my
    thanks to-day.

Now much have I found to be glad of, much have I
    sorrowed for,
But naught is better to hear than the foot of a friend
    at the door;
And naught is better to feel than the touch of a sister
    hand
That says, "What are words between us — I know and
    may understand."

For the friendship of true women, Lord, that hath
    lasted since time began,
That is deeper far and finer far than the friendship of
    man to man;

For the tie of a kinship wonderful that holds us as
      blood-bonds may —
For the friendship of true women, Lord, take you my
      thanks to-day.

Many the joys I have welcomed, many the joys that
      have passed,
But this is the good unfailing and this is the peace that
      shall last;
From love that dies and love that lies and love that
      must cling and sting
Back to the arms of our sisters we turn for our com-
      forting.

For the friendship of true women, Lord, that hath been
      and ever shall be
Since a woman stood at a woman's side at the cross of
      Calvary;
For the tears we weep and the trusts we keep and the
      self-same prayers we pray —
For the friendship of true women, Lord, take you my
      thanks to-day.

                        — Theodosia Garrison.

      Love, a plant of fragile form,
      Fired by ardent suns to birth,
      Shrinks before the whelming storm,
      Withering, dies and sinks to earth.
      Friendship, like a nobler river,
      Rolls its stately waters by;
      Tempest tossed and troubled never,
      Gliding to eternity.
                    — Henry George Bohn.

A Lost Friend

Your soul, that for years I have counted
    An open book, read to the end,
Is lettered all strange, since a lover
    Looks out from the eyes of a friend.

The white pages now are turned rosy,
    The chapters are numbered anew,
The old plot is lost, and the hero
    Who, up to last night, was just you —

Just dear old friend Jack, and no other,
    To-night is a stranger, I vow;
And though I am fain to be gracious,
    The truth is, I scarcely know how.

Where now is your celibate gospel?
    What now of Love's follies and faults?
Refuted last night when your lips, sir,
    Chasséed o'er my cheek in the waltz.

Life-faith we swore, friendly fraternal
    To keep it—ah me! half a year,
And I, Chloris now to your Strephon,
    Accept my new role with a tear, —

A tear for the dear old days ended,
    A tear for the friend lost for ay,
For careless old comradeship fleeing
    For ever before Love to-day.

Dear, read me aright! Though words falter,
    And lips prove but dumb, your heart hears;
The Jack of to-day I love truly,
    Yet oh, for the Jack of old years!

                    — Minnie Gilmore.

A Temple to Friendship

"A Temple to Friendship," said Laura, enchanted,
  "I 'll build in this garden, — the thought is divine!"
Her temple was built, and she now only wanted
  An image of Friendship to place on the shrine.
She flew to a sculptor, who set down before her
  A Friendship, the fairest his art could invent;
But so cold and so dull, that the youthful adorer
  Saw plainly this was not the idol she mean.

"O never," she cried, "could I think of enshrining
  An image whose looks are so joyless and dim: —
But yon little god, upon roses reclining,
  We 'll make, if you please, sir, a Friendship of him."
So the bargain was struck: with the little god laden
  She joyfully flew to her shrine in the grove;
"Farewell," said the sculptor, "you 're not the first
    maiden
  Who came but for Friendship and took away Love."
                              — Thomas Moore.

We Have Been Friends Together

We have been friends together,
  In sunshine and in shade;
  Since first beneath the chestnut trees
  In infancy we played.
But coldness dwells within thy heart,
  A cloud is on thy brow;
We have been friends together —
  Shall a light word part us now?

We have been gay together;
  We have laughed at little jests;

For the font of hope was gushing
  Warm and joyous in our breasts.
But laughter now hath fled thy lip,
  And sullen glooms thy brow;
We have been gay together —
  Shall a light word part us now?

We have been sad together,
  We have wept with bitter tears,
O'er the grass-grown graves, where slumbered
  The hopes of early years.
The voices which are silent there
  Would bid thee clear thy brow;
We have been sad together —
  Oh! what shall part us now?

— Caroline Elizabeth Sarah Norton.

Friendship After Years

The March winds bring to bloom the anemone,
  The violets prove April in the sky,
  To fields of May a myriad beauties fly,
June roses tune the world to harmony:
We smile, and take these joyous gifts as free —
  Unheeding; yet how precious to the eye
  Are roses after snow; and when the sun on high
Makes flowers of the frost, 't is wizardry!

Youth hath his friendships dear, unsought, unwon,
  And takes them as he takes the thought of spring
  When spring is self, as rightful heritage;
But friendship after years is like the sun
  In frost, the rose in winter blossoming:
  And oh, the friends of youth, how dear in age!

— Wallace Rice.

34

Ballade of a Woman's Friendship

Eyes as gray as a plover's wing,
  Fine-spun hair with a dash of red,
Fresh her lips as the breath of spring,
  When from swaying violets shed —
  Ah! and the poise of her dainty head,
Such enchantment as it could lend.
  Test her? test but a spider's thread,
She was a woman, not a friend.

Light she moved with a graceful swing,
  Strength and ease in the motion wed,
Down through the summer's wakening
  Daisies under her footsteps spread,
  The swallow passed like an arrow sped
Over the river's brawling bend:
  Who shall mourn for a trust that fled?
She was a woman, not a friend.

Low her voice as the shells that sing,
  Soft on a shore-line's sandy bed,
Hope's fair buds she could blithely bring;
  Yet, and yet if you asked for bread,
  Then she would give you a stone instead,
Fail you when you would most depend:
  After all had been done and said,
She was a woman, not a friend.

  Prince! a health to the heart that bled,
I her beauty and worth defend:
  Why should a man be thus misled?
She was a woman, not a friend.

—— Ernest McGaffey.

35

As for Me, I Have a Friend

Let the sower scatter seed
  Where the crumbling furrows blend;
Let the churchman praise his creed,
  The beginning and the end;
  As for me, I have a friend.

Does the sun forget to shine
  And the wind blow sere and chill?
Does the cluster leave the vine,
  And the ice begird the rill?
  I shall rest contented still.

Must the rose be stripped of leaf
  When the waning June has passed?
Shall an autumn voice its grief
  In the lone November blast?
  What of that? — a friend will last.

Why should I, then, make complaint
  To the days that round me roll?
She my missal is, and saint,
  Clad in womanhood's white stole,
  She, the keeper of my soul.

Not love's chalice to my lips,
  Not that bitter draught she brings,
Which, as Hybla's honey drips
  And like bosomed asp-worm stings,
  No! she tells of happier things.

Simple friendship, just that much
  To enfold me as a strand

Of her hair might; and the touch
  Of a gracious welcoming hand
  That I grasp, and understand.

Let death ope or lock his gate
  Let the lilies break or bend,
And the iron will of fate
  Sorrows now or fortune send, —
  As for me, I have a friend.

                — Ernest McGaffey.

Platonic

I had sworn to be a bachelor, she had sworn to be
  a maid,
For we quite agreed in doubting whether matrimony
  paid,
Besides, we had our higher loves — fair science ruled
  my heart,
And she said her young affections were all wound
  up in art.

So we laughed at those wise men who say that friendship cannot live
'Twixt man and woman unless each has something
  more to give:
We would be friends, and friends as true as e'er
  were man and man;
I 'd be a second David and she Miss Jonathan.

We scorned all sentimental trash, — vows, kisses, tears,
  and sighs;
High friendship, such as ours, might well such childish
  arts despise;
We liked each other, that was all, quite all there was
  to say,

So we just shook hands upon it, in a business sort
of way.

We shared our secrets and our joys, together hoped
and feared,
With common purpose sought the goal that young
Ambition reared;
We dreamed together of the days, the dream-bright
days to come;
We were strictly confidential and we called each
other "chum."

And many a day we wandered together o'er the hills,
I seeking bugs and butterflies, and she the ruined mills
And rustic bridges and the like, that picture-makers
prize
To run in with their waterfalls, and groves, and
summer skies.

And many a quiet evening in hours of silent ease
We floated down the river, or strolled beneath the
trees,
And talked in long gradation from the poets to the
weather,
While the western skies and my cigar burned slowly
out together.

Yet through it all no whispered word, no tell-tale
glance or sigh,
Told aught of warmer sentiment than friendly sympathy,
We talked of love as coolly as we talked of nebulæ,
And thought no more of being one than we did of
being three.

"Well, good bye, chum!" I took her hand, for the
    time had come to go,
My going meant our parting, when to meet, we did
    not know.
I had lingered long and said farewell with a very
    heavy heart;
For although we were but friends 't is hard for honest
    friends to part.

"Good bye, old fellow! don't forget your friends
    beyond the sea,
And some day when you 've lots of time, drop a line
    or two to me."
The words came lightly, gayly, but a great sob, just
    behind,
Welled upward with a story of quite a different kind.

And she raised her eyes to mine,— great liquid eyes
    of blue,
Filled to the brim, and running o'er, like violet cups
    of dew,
One long, long glance, and then I did what I never
    did before —
Perhaps the tears meant friendship, but I 'm sure the
    kiss meant more.

                        — William B. Terrett.

Song

The ripest fruit is the fruit that hangs too high,
The truest friend is the friend we never find,
The dearest hour is the hour we say good bye,
The darling hope is the hope we leave behind.
                      — William Theodore Peters.

To a Friend

When we were idlers with the loitering rills,
  The need of human love we little noted:
  Our love was nature; and the peace that floated
  On the white mist, and dwelt upon the hills,
To one accord subdued our wayward wills:
  One soul was ours, one mind, one heart devoted,
  That, wisely doating, asked not why it doated,
  And ours the unknown joy, which knowing kills.

But now I find how dear thou wert to me;
  That man is more than half of nature's treasure,
  Of that fair beauty which no eye can see,
Of that sweet music which no ear can measure;
  And now the streams may sing for others' pleasure,
  The hills sleep on in their eternity.

> — Hartley Coleridge.

Dreams, hopes — bubbles, butterflies all,
  That, in chasing, we find —
Not always delusion — but truth,
  The gold of heart and mind.
There is wisdom, my dear, in this:
  To know where rainbows end,
And, digging there, bring up to light —
  The pity of a friend.

> — Charles G. Blanden.

If you no longer love me,
  To friendship why pretend?
Unworthy was the lover,
  Unworthy be the friend.

> — Walter Savage Landor.

A Friend

Thy face, my friend, is graven on my heart,
Traced by the finger of that Wingless Love
That draws a man unto his friend with bonds
Not lightly to be sundered.

                       Still I sit
Beneath the single lamp's well-tempered glow;
I hear the roaring of the tameless night,
The rattle of the unencountered latch,
But thou art gone. Thy place beneath our lamp
Is empty; and my life is empty, too.
Men come and go, and for some little space
They call me friend, unweening what they say;
But thou art gone, and still I sit alone.
The book slips from my hand, and to mine eyes,
Heavy and dim with pages turned in vain,
A vision rises of thy kindly face,
My heart is filled with a strange sense of hope,
My hand goes forth to touch thee,

                            Thou art gone.
The small, sharp crackling of thine empty chair
Brings back the cruel sense of loneliness,
For thou art gone indeed, and I alone
Must bear my burden to the hopeless end.

              — Gaillard Thomas Lapsley.

To My Old Friend, William Leachman

Fer forty year and better you have been a friend to me,
Through days of sore afflictions and dire adversity,
You allus had a kind word of counsul to impart,
Which was like a healin' 'intment to the sorrow of my
        hart.

When I burried my first womern, William Leachman,
    it was you
Had the only consolation that I could listen to —
For I knowed you had gone through it and had rallied
    from the blow,
And when you said I 'd do the same, I knowed you 'd
    ort to know.

But that time I 'll long remember; how I wundered
    here and thare —
Through the settin'-room and kitchen, and out in the
    open air —
And the snowflakes whirlin', whirlin', and the fields
    a frozen glare,
And the neighbors' sleds and wagons congergatin'
    ev'rywhare.

I turned my eyes to'rds heaven, but the sun was hid
    away;
I turned my eyes to'rds earth again, but all was cold
    and gray;
And the clock, like ice a-crackin', clickt the icy hours
    in two —
And my eyes 'd never thawed out ef it had n't been
    fer you !

We set thare by the smoke-house — me and you out
    thare alone —
Me a-thinkin' — you a-talkin' in a soothin' under-
    tone —
You a-talkin' — me a-thinkin' of the summers long ago,
And a-writin' ''Marthy — Marthy'' with my finger in
    the snow !

William Leachman, I can see you jest as plane as I
      could then;
And your hand is on my shoulder, and you rouse
      me up again;
And I see the tears a-drippin' from your own eyes, as
      you say:
"Be rickonciled and bear it — we but linger fer a
      day!" . . .

Ways was devius, William Leachman, that me and you
      has past;
But as I found you true at first, I find you true at last;
And, now the time 's a-comin' mighty nigh our jour-
      ney's end,
I want to throw wide open all my soul to you, my
      friend. . . .

                   — James Whitcomb Riley.

It 's an owercome sooth for age an' youth
    And it brooks wi' nae denial,
That the dearest friends are the auldest friends
    And the young are just on trial.

There 's a rival bauld wi' young an' auld
    And it 's him that has bereft me;
For the surest friends are the auldest friends
    And the maist o' mine hae left me.

There are kind hearts still, for friends to fill
    And fools to take and break them;
But the nearest friends are the auldest friends
    And the grave 's the place to seek them.

                   — Robert Louis Stevenson.

Bill and Joe

Come, dear old comrade, you and I
Will steal an hour from days gone by,
The shining days when life was new,
And all was bright with morning dew,
The lusty days of long ago,
When you were Bill and I was Joe.

Your name may flaunt a titled trail
Proud as a cockerel's rainbow tail,
And mine as brief appendix wear
As Tam O'Shanter's luckless mare;
To-day, old friend, remember still
That I am Joe and you are Bill.

You 've won the world's great envied prize,
And grand you look in people's eyes,
With **H.O.N.** and **L.L.D.**
In big brave letters fair to see, —
Your fist, old fellow! off they go! —
How are you, Bill? How are you, Joe?

You 've won the judge's ermined robe;
You 've taught your name to half the globe;
You 've sung mankind a deathless strain;
You 've made the dead past live again:
The world may call you what it will
But you and I are Joe and Bill.

The chaffing young folks stare and say
"See those old buffers, bent and gray, —
They talk like fellows in their teens!
Mad, poor old boys! That 's what it means," —
And shake their heads; they little know
The throbbing hearts of Bill and Joe! —

How Bill forgets his hour of pride,
And Joe sits smiling at his side;
How Joe, in spite of time's disguise,
Finds the old schoolmate in his eyes, —
Those calm, stern eyes that melt and fill
As Joe looks fondly up at Bill.

Ah, pensive scholar, what is fame?
A fitful tongue of leaping flame;
A giddy whirlwind's fickle gust,
That lifts a pinch of mortal dust;
A few swift years, and who can show
Which dust was Bill and which was Joe?

The weary idol takes his stand,
Holds out his bruised and aching hand,
While gaping thousands come and go, —
How vain it seems, this empty show!
Till all at once his pulses thrill; —
'T is poor old Joe's "God bless you, Bill!"

And shall we breathe in happier spheres
The names that pleased our mortal ears;
In some sweet lull of harp and song
For earth-born spirits none too long,
Just whispering of the world below
Where this was Bill and that was Joe?

No matter; while our home is here
No sounding name is half so dear;
When fades at length our lingering day,
Who cares what pompous tombstones say?
Read on the hearts that love us still,
Hic jacet Joe. Hic jacet Bill.

          — Oliver Wendell Holmes.

Wingless Love

A firefly glimmering hither and yon, —
   A buttefly's hesitant enterprise
Among the flowers July shines on, —
Love is a sprite, and away he flies;
   But, sweeter than blossoms, the seed supplies
Life and hope and imaginings
   Still to endure when summer dies:
Friendship is Love without his wings.

Fluttering now above Helicon;
   Now from Arcadia Cupid hies;
Psyche is left alone and wan —
   Love is a sprite, and away he flies;
   Yet David on Jonathan still relies,
Still to Damon Pythias clings,
   Nothing a friend to a friend denies —
Friendship is Love without his wings.

Unstable as any moon that 's shone, —
   Unquiet as clouds when the curlew cries, —
Unsure as the tides, now here, now gone, —
   Love is a sprite, and away he flies;
   But there is a haven of certainties,
The best and safest a long life brings,
   With Hope and Heaven his close allies,
Friendship is Love without his wings.

O Prince! uncertain is April's skies,
   Love is a sprite, and away he flies;
While close to the heart the spirit sings,
"Friendship is Love without his wings."

                 — John Jarvis Holden.

A Woman Friend

Song have I known, and women and wine;
Laughter and pleasure, long were they mine;
Days full of sunlight, nights without end —
But give me, for comfort, a good woman friend!

Long did I seek and often I found
Joy and delight and mirth without bound;
These have I known, all these have I passed —
Seeking a good woman's friendship at last.

Pleasure is fickle, Mirth is a jade,
Love is the jest of a light-hearted maid;
Happiness lasts — what use to pretend! —
Safe in the heart of a good woman friend.

Merriment 's sweet, but its goblet must spill;
Laughter is lovely, smiles fairer still:
Sympathy 's best, understanding complete,
And a good woman's friendship life's last and best
    sweet.

Take all the rest, the laughter, the kiss —
These have I loved, yet these I 'll not miss;
Leave the affection years cannot scathe,
A good woman's friendship, more holy than Faith.

Clara, though springtide is fair, summer dear,
Autumn has brought me the crown of my year;
Keep for me warmth against winter, and take
This guerdon of friendship for Happiness' sake.

— Wallace Rice.

From "The Meadows in Spring"

'T is a dull sight
  To see the year dying,
When winter winds
  Set the yellow wood sighing.
    Sighing, oh! sighing.

When such a time cometh,
  I do retire
Into a bright room
  Beside a bright fire:
    Oh, pile a bright fire! . . .

Then with an old friend
  I talk of our youth —
How 't was gladsome, but often
  Foolish, forsooth:
    But gladsome, gladsome!

Or to get merry
  We sing some old rhyme,
That made the wood ring again
  In summer time —
    Sweet summer time!

Then go we to smoking,
  Silent and snug:
Nought passes between us,
  Save a brown jug —
    Sometimes!

And sometimes a tear
  Will rise in each eye,

Seeing the two old friends
So merrily —
So merrily!

And ere we go to bed,
Go we, go we,
Down on the ashes
We kneel on the knee,
Praying together!

Thus, then live I,
Till, 'mid all the gloom,
By Heaven! the bold sun
Is with me in the room,
Shining, shining! . . .

— Edward FitzGerald.

An Honest Old Friend

With an honest old friend and a merry old song,
And a flask of old port, let me sit the night long,
And laugh at the malice of those who repine
That they must drink porter whilst I can drink wine.

I envy no mortal though ever so great,
Nor scorn I a wretch for his lowly estate;
But what I abhor and esteem as a curse,
Is poorness of spirit, not poorness of purse.

Then dare to be generous, dauntless, and gay,
Let us merrily pass life's remainder away;
Upheld by our friends, we our foes may despise,
For the more we are envied, the higher we rise.

— Henry Carey.

From "Under the Willows"

In June 't is good to lie beneath a tree
While the blithe season comforts every sense,
Steeps all the brain in rest, and heals the heart,
Brimming it o'er with sweetness unawares,
Fragrant and silent as that rosy snow
Wherewith the pitying apple tree fills up
And tenderly lines some last-year robin's nest.
There muse I of old times, old hopes, old friends,—
Old friends! the writing of those words has borne
My fancy backward to the gracious past,
The generous past, when all was possible,
For all was then untried; the years between
Have taught some sweet, some bitter lessons, none
Wiser than this,— to spend in all things else,
But of old friends to be most miserly.
Each year to ancient friendship adds a ring,
As to an oak, and precious more and more,
Without deservingness or help of ours,
They grow, and, silent, wider spread, each year,
Their unbought ring of shelter or of shade.

— James Russell Lowell.

Give a friend your heart,
  Hold it from your lover;
Quick to heal love's smart,
Give your friend your heart;
His the better part
  Soon must you discover;
Give a friend your heart,
  Hold it from your lover.

— John Jarvis Holden.

Old Friends

We just shake hands at meeting
  With many that come nigh,
We nod the head in greeting
  To many that go by.
But we welcome through the gateway
  Our few old friends and true;
Then hearts leap up and straightway
  There 's open house for you,
    Old friends, wide-open house for you.

The surface will be sparkling,
  Let but a sunbeam shine,
But in the deep lies darkling
  The true life of the wine.
The froth is for the many,
  The wine is for the few;
Unseen, untouched of any,
  We keep the best for you,
    Old friends, the very best for you.

''The many'' cannot know us,
  They only pace the strand
Where at our worst we show us,
  The waters thick as sand;
But out beyond the leaping
  Dim surge 't is clear and blue,
And there, old friends, we 're keeping
  A waiting calm for you,
    Old friends, a sacred calm for you.
             — Gerald Massey.

Oh, be my friend, and teach me to be thine.
            — Ralph Waldo Emerson.

To a Distant Friend

Why art thou silent! Is thy love a plant
  Of such weak fiber that the treacherous air
  Of absence withers what was once so fair?
  Is there no debt to pay, no boon to grant?
Yet have my thoughts for thee been vigilant,
  Bound to thy service with unceasing care —
  The mind's least generous wish a mendicant
For nought but what thy happiness could spare.

Speak! — though this soft warm heart, once free to hold
  A thousand tender pleasures, thine and mine,
  Be left more desolate, more dreary cold
Than a forsaken bird's nest filled with snow
  'Mid its own bush of leafless eglantine —
  Speak, that my torturing doubts their end may know!
                              — William Wordsworth.

An Epitaph

Of our great love, Parthenophil,
This little stone abideth still
    Sole sign and token.
I seek thee yet, and yet shall seek
Though faint mine eyes, my spirit weak
    With prayers unspoken.

Meanwhile best friend of friends, do thou,
If this the cruel fates allow,
    By death's dark river,
Among those shadowy people, drink
No drop for me on Lethe's brink:
    Forget me never!

The Solace of Friends

When care is on me, earth a wilderness,
   The evening starless and unsunned the day,
   When I go clouded like them, sad and gray,
   My fears grown mighty and my hope grown less;
When every lilting tune brings new distress,
   Unmirthful sound the children at their play,
   Nor any book can charm my thought away
   From the deep sense of mine unworthiness;
Then think I on my friends. Such friends have I,
   Witty and wise, learnéd, affectionate,
   There must be in me something fine and high
To hold such treasures at the hands of fate;
   Their nobleness hints my nobility,
   Their love arrays my soul in robes of state.
                    — Wallace Rice.

From a Window

Through dusky etchings of the wood
    The white snows glow,
The tree arms, twined in sisterhood,
    Together grow.
    Brown grasses dead
Beside the tree trunks lie;
    Clear overhead
Bends down the tender sky,
And in my heart, O friend, a thought of thee!
O world of God, thou art so dear to me!
                 — Charles T. Sempers.

They take the sunshine from the world who take
friendship from life.

My Friend, Adown Life's Valley

My friend, adown Life's valley, hand in hand,
  With grateful change of grave and merry speech
  Or song, our hearts unlocking each to each,
  We 'll journey onward to the silent land;
And when stern Death shall loose that loving band,
  Taking in his cold hand a hand of ours,
  The one shall strew the other's grave with flowers,
  Nor shall his heart a moment be unmanned.

My friend and brother! if thou goest first,
  Wilt thou no more revisit me below?
  Yea, when my heart seems happy causelessly
And swells, not dreaming why, as it would burst
  With joy unspeakable — my soul shall know
  That thou, unseen, art bending over me.
                              — James Russell Lowell.

To a Friend

Fast as the rolling seasons bring
    The hour fate to those we love,
Each pearl that leaves the broken string
    Is set in Friendship's crown above.
As narrower grows the earthy chain,
    The circle widens in the sky;
These are our treasures that remain,
    But those are stars that beam on high.
                        — Oliver Wendell Holmes.

Great souls by instinct to each other turn,
Demand alliance, and in friendship burn.
                              — Joseph Addison.

From "Oft in the Stilly Night"

When I remember all
The friends, so linked together,
  I 've seen around me fall,
Like leaves in wintry weather;
  I feel like one
  Who treads alone
Some banquet-hall deserted,
  Whose lights are fled,
  Whose garlands dead,
And all but he departed!
  Thus, in the stilly night,
  Ere Slumber's chain has bound me,
Sad Memory brings the light
Of other days around me.
                        — Thomas Moore.

The leaves are falling; so am I:
The few late flowers have moisture in the eye;
        So have I too.
  Scarcely on any bough is heard
  Joyous, or even unjoyous, bird
        The whole wood through.
Winter may come: he brings but nigher
His circle (yearly narrowing) to the fire
        Where old friends meet:
  Let him; — now heaven is overcast,
  And spring and summer both are past,
        And all things sweet.
                    — Walter Savage Landor.

I count myself in nothing else so happy
As in a soul remembering my good friends.
                    — William Shakespeare.

On the Death of Drake

Green be the turf above thee,
　　Friend of my better days!
None knew thee but to love thee,
　　Nor named thee but to praise.

Tears fell when thou wert dying,
　　From eyes unused to weep,
And long, where thou art lying,
　　Will tears the cold turf steep.

When hearts, whose truth was proven,
　　Like thine, are laid in earth,
There should a wreath be woven
　　To tell the world their worth;

And I who woke each morrow
　　To clasp thy hand in mine,
Who shared thy joy and sorrow,
　　Whose weal and woe were thine;

It should be mine to braid it
　　Around thy faded brow,
But I 've in vain essayed it,
　　And feel I cannot now.

While memory bids me weep thee,
　　Nor thoughts nor words are free, —
The grief is fixed too deeply
　　That mourns a man like thee.
　　　　　　　　— Fitz-Greene Halleck.

Even Heaven is sweeter for friends gone before.

May and Death

I wish that when you died last May,
  Charles, there had died along with you
Three parts of spring's delightful things;
  Aye, and for me the fourth part too.

A foolish thought, and worse, perhaps!
  There must be many a pair of friends
Who arm-in-arm deserve the warm
  Moon-births and the long evening-ends.

So, for their sake, be May still May!
  Let their new time, as mine of old,
Do all it did for me; I bid
  Sweet sights and sounds throng manifold.

Only one little sight, one plant
  Woods have in May, that starts up green
Save a sole streak which, so to speak,
  Is Spring's blood, spilt its leaves between —

That, they might spare; a certain wood
  Might miss the plant; their loss was small;
But I — whene'er the leaf grows there —
  Its drop comes from my heart, that 's all.
                          — Robert Browning.

Large was his bounty, and his soul sincere;
  Heaven did a recompense as largely send;
He gave to misery — all he had — a tear;
  He gained from Heaven — 't was all he wished — a
    friend.
                          — Thomas Gray.

57

Departed Friends

They are all gone into the world of light!
    And I alone sit lingering here!
Their very memory is fair and bright,
    And my sad thoughts doth clear.

It glows and glitters in my cloudy breast
    Like stars upon some gloomy grove,
Or those faint beams in which this hill is dressed
    After the Sun's remove.

I see them walking in an air of glory,
    Whose light doth trample on my days;
My days, which are at best but dull and hoary,
    Mere glimmering and decays.

O holy Hope! and high Humility!
    High as the Heavens above;
These are your walks, and you have showed them me
    To kindle my cold love.

Dear, beauteous death; the Jewel of the Just!
    Shining no where but in the dark;
What mysteries do lie beyond thy dust,
    Could man outlook that mark!

He that hath found some fledged bird's nest may know
    At first sight if the bird be flown;
But what fair dell or grove he sings in now,
    That is to him unknown.

And yet, as Angels in some brighter dreams
    Call to the soul when man doth sleep.
So some strange thoughts transcend our wonted themes,
    And into glory peep.

If a star were confined into a tomb,
  Her captive flames must needs burn there;
But when the hand that locked her up gives room
  She 'll shine through all the sphere.

O father of eternal life, and all
  Created glories under thee!
Resume thy spirit from this world of thrall
  Into true liberty!

Either disperse these mists, which blot and fill
  My perspective still as they pass:
Or else remove me hence unto that hill,
  Where I shall need no glass.

— Henry Vaughan.

For friendship, of itself a holy tie,
Is made more sacred by adversity.

— John Dryden.

When Shall We Three Meet Again?

When shall we three meet again?
When shall we three meet again?
Oft shall glowing hope expire,
Oft shall wearied love retire,
Oft shall death and sorrow reign,
Ere we three shall meet again.

Though in distant lands we sigh,
Parched beneath a hostile sky;
Though the deep between us rolls, —
Friendship shall unite our souls,
Still, in Fancy's rich domain
Oft shall we three meet again.

L'Amitee est l'Amour sans Ailes

Why should my anxious breast repine,
  Because my youth is fled?
Days of delight may still be mine;
  Affection is not dead,
In tracing back the years of youth,
One firm record, one lasting truth,
  Celestial consolation brings;
Bear it, ye breezes, to the seat,
Where first my heart responsive beat, —
    "Friendship is Love without his wings!"

Through few, but deeply checquered years,
  What moments have been mine!
Now half obscured by clouds of tears,
  Now bright in rays divine;
Howe'er my future doom be cast,
My soul enraptured with the past,
  To one idea fondly clings;
Friendship! that thought is all thine own,
Worth worlds of bliss, that thought alone —
    "Friendship is Love without his wings!" . . .

Oh, Love! before thy glowing shrine
  My early vows were paid;
My hopes, my dreams, my heart was thine,
  But these are now decayed;
For thine are pinions like the wind.
No trace of thee remains behind,
  Except, alas! thy jealous stings.
Away, away! delusive power,
Thou shalt not haunt my coming hour;
  Unless, indeed, without thy wings.

60

Seat of my youth! thy distant spire
   Recalls each scene of joy:
My bosom glows with former fire, —
   In mind again a boy.
Thy grove of elms, thy verdant hill,
Thy very path delight me still,
   Each flower a double fragrance flings;
Again, as once, in converse gay,
Each dear associate seems to say,
   "Friendship is Love without his wings!"

My Lycus! wherefore dost thou weep?
   Thy falling tears restrain;
Affection for a time may sleep,
   But, oh, 't will wake again.
Think, think, my friend, when next we meet
Our long-wished interview, how sweet!
   From this my hope of rapture springs;
While youthful hearts thus fondly swell,
Absence, my friend, can only tell,
   "Friendship is Love without his wings!"

Fictions and dreams inspire the bard
   Who rolls the epic song;
Friendship and truth be my reward —
   To me no bays belong;
If laureled Fame but dwells with lies,
Me the enchantress ever flies,
   Whose heart and not whose fancy sings.
Simple and young, I dare not feign;
Mine be the rude yet heartfelt strain.
   "Friendship is Love without his wings!"

                    —Byron.

Counsel

If thou shouldst bid thy friend farewell,
　　But for one night though that farewell may be,
Press thou his hand in thine; thou canst not tell
　　How far from thee

Fate or caprice may lead his feet
　　Ere that to-morrow come.　Men have been known
Lightly to turn the corner of a street,
　　And days have grown

To months, and months to lagging years,
　　Before they look on loving eyes again.
Parting, at best, is underlaid with tears,
　　With tears and pain,

Therefore, lest sudden death should come between,
　　Or time, or distance, clasp with pressure true
The palm of him who goeth forth; unseen,
　　Fate goeth too!

Yea, find thou alway time to say
　　Some earnest word betwixt the idle talk,
Lest with thee henceforth ever, night and day,
　　Regret should walk.

　　　　　　　　　　　　—Mary E. M. Davis.

Acknowledgment

The thanks of the compilers are due to Mrs. Ella Wheeler Wilcox and Messrs. W. B. Conkey Company for permission to use "Friendship"; to Mrs. Theodosia Garrison and Mr. Mitchell Kennerley for "A Thanksgiving", from "The Joy of Life"; to Miss Caroline Duer for "Count Me Not Less"; to Mr. Charles G. Blanden for "Dreams and Hopes"; to Mr. Bliss Carman for the extract from "The Joys of the Road"; to Mr. Sam Walter Foss and Messrs. The Lothrop, Lee Shepard Company for "The House by the Side of the Road"; to Messrs. Forbes & Company for the late Ben King's "I Like the New Friends Best"; to Mr. Ernest McGaffey for "Ballade of a Woman's Friendship" and "As for Me, I Have a Friend"; and to Mr. James Whitcomb Riley and Messrs. The Bobbs-Merrill Company, owners of the copyright, for "To My Old Friend, William Leachman"

The Little Book Series

Edited and Compiled
by
Wallace and Frances Rice

The Little Book of Love
The Little Book of Kisses
The Little Book of Friendship
The Little Book of Brides
The Little Book of Sports
The Little Book of Out-of-Doors
The Little Book of Cheer
The Little Book of Lullabies
The Little Book of Laughter
The Little Book of Limericks
The Little Book of School-Days
The Little Book of Bohemia

Made in three styles as follows:

Half-vellum, gold and colored paper sides, boxed, per vol.,		35 cents
Booklovers' edition, cartridge paper sides .	" "	60 cents
Flexible Morocco leather	" "	$1.00

The Little Books are sold everywhere or will be sent postpaid
on receipt of price, by the

Publishers   The Reilly & Britton Co.   Chicago

Complete catalogue sent, postpaid, on request

The
LITTLE BOOK
SERIES